THE SIERRA CLUB
MOUNTAIN LIGHT POSTCARD COLLECTION

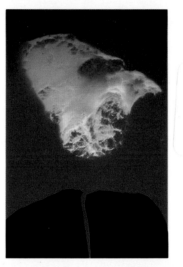

A PORTFOLIO BY GALEN ROWELL

Sierra Club Books

The Sierra Club, founded in 1892 by John Muir, has devoted itself to the study and protection of the earth's scenic and ecological resources—mountains, wetlands, woodlands, wild shores and rivers, deserts and plains. The publishing program of the Sierra Club offers books to the public as a nonprofit educational service in the hope that they may enlarge the public's understanding of the Club's basic concerns. The point of view expressed in each book, however, does not necessarily represent that of the Club. The Sierra Club has some sixty chapters coast to coast, in Canada, Hawaii, and Alaska. For information about how you may participate in its programs to preserve wilderness and the quality of life, please address inquiries to Sierra Club, 730 Polk Street, San Francisco, CA 94109.

This collection is based on the book *Mountain Light,* which was produced in association with the publisher at the Yolla Bolly Press, Covelo, California.

Library of Congress Cataloging-in-Publication Data

Rowell, Galen A.
  The Sierra Club Mountain light postcard collection.

  Thirty color images from: Mountain light. c1986.
  1. Postcards—United States. 2. United States in art. 3. Sierra Club. I. Rowell, Galen A. Mountain light. II. Sierra Club. III. Title.
  NC1877.S54R68   1987   741.68′3′0924   87–13201
  0–87156–779–2

Book design by Bonnie Smetts
Printed by Dai Nippon Printing Company, Ltd., Tokyo, Japan

10 9 8 7 6 5 4 3 2

Magic Hour

Twice each day the cool, blue light of night interacts with the warm tones of daylight. Luckily for color photographers, these events, though predictable, are not consistent. For a full hour at either end of the day colors of light mix together in endless combinations, as if someone in the sky were shaking a kaleidoscope. This effect takes place, not directly where the sun rises or sets, but where the sun's rays beam warm, direct light onto parts of the land and sky that are also lit by the cool, reflected light of evening.

The most interesting parts of the natural world are the edges, places where ocean meets land, meadow meets forest, timberline touches the heights. These geographical edges excite scientists in much the same way that edges of light fascinate me. Near the end of the day, transmitted light becomes ever warmer, reflected light ever colder. I look for this visual edge, especially where it is emphasized against clouds and other light backgrounds. In fact, my favorite way to photograph a geographical edge is to make it converge with a visual edge of light that will underscore the difference between the two zones.

Most amateur photographers think of landscapes simply as objects to be photographed. They tend to forget that they are never photographing an object, but rather light itself. Where there is no light, they will have no picture; where there is remarkable light, they *may* have a remarkable picture. When the magic hour arrives, my thoughts center on light rather than on the landscape.

I search for perfect light, then hunt for something earthbound to match it with. The best images that result from this process look like visual riddles with unexpected answers; and like verbal riddles, visual riddles have been created by starting with the answers then working backward.

When the light is right and everything is working for me, I feel as tense as when making a difficult maneuver high on a mountain. A minute — and sometimes mere seconds — can make the difference between a superb image and a mundane one.

—Galen Rowell, from *Mountain Light: In Search of the Dynamic Landscape*

Galen Rowell's work has been published in *Audubon, National Geographic, Sports Illustrated, Sierra, Popular Photography,* and the Sierra Club calendars, among others. His photographs have been exhibited at New York's International Center of Photography and the Smithsonian Institution, as well as in galleries throughout the United States.

Mr. Rowell has participated in more than 1,000 climbs on four continents, and in more than ten major expeditions in the Himalaya during the course of his mountaineering career. He is the author/photographer of six previous books, including MOUNTAINS OF THE MIDDLE KINGDOM, IN THE THRONE ROOM OF THE MOUNTAIN GODS, and, with John McPhee, ALASKA: IMAGES OF THE COUNTRY.

Trango Towers, Karakoram Himalaya, Pakistan.

Lynx in alpine flowers, Teklanika River, Alaska Range.

Water streaks on Quarter Domes, Yosemite, California.

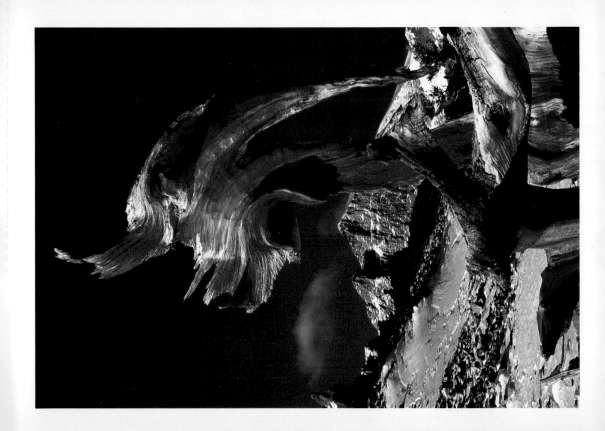

Bristlecone snag under Wheeler Peak, Snake Range,
Nevada.

Moonrise, Sherwin Plateau, Eastern Sierra, California.

Sunrise over the Skeena River, British Columbia, Canada.

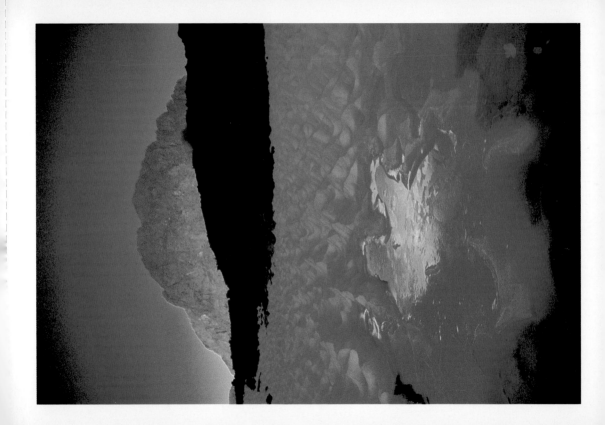

Late summer snow under Mount Williamson, southern
Sierra, California.

Moonset at sunrise, Wheeler Crest, Eastern Sierra,
California.

Jeffrey pine and juniper on Olmsted Point, Yosemite,
California.

Sunset after a storm, Yosemite Valley, California.

Big Bird Lake, Sequoia National Park, California.

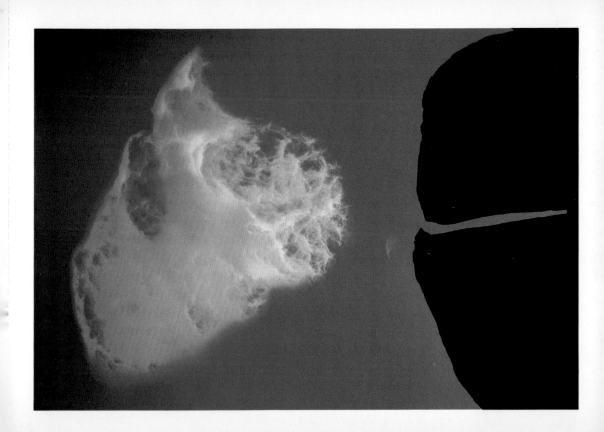

Split rock and cloud, Eastern Sierra, California.

Riders beneath giant sand dune, Pamir Range, China.

Cloud cap on K2, Karakoram Himalaya, Pakistan.

Summer flowers in sagebrush meadow, Grant Lake,
California.

Vermilion Lakes, Canadian Rockies.

Rainbow over the Potala Palace, Lhasa, Tibet.

Valley of the Ten Peaks, Banff Park, Canadian Rockies.

Clearing storm over El Capitan, Yosemite, California.

Bouldering near Bishop in the Eastern Sierra, California.

Cirque of the Unclimbables, Logan Mountains,
Northwest Territories, Canada.

California bighorn rams in the High Sierra, California.

Fall storm over Yosemite Valley, California.

Pool below Anye Machin, northeastern Tibet.

Dawn on Sentinel Pass Trail, Canadian Rockies.

Porters at Concordia, Karakoram Himalaya, Pakistan.

The Sierra Club MOUNTAIN LIGHT Postcard Collection.
Copyright © 1986 by Galen Rowell/Mountain Light, Inc.

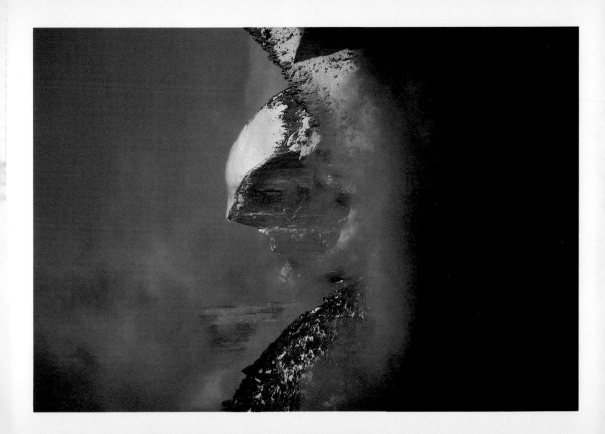

Yosemite Valley in winter, California.

Cabin in the Don Sheldon Amphitheater, Alaska Range.

Three climbers on Mount Everest's West Ridge at
24,500 feet, Tibet.

Sunrise on Tioga Pass, High Sierra, California.